Be the Change! Shaping Your Community

Be a
MENTOR!

By Kate Mikoley

Gareth Stevens
PUBLISHING

Please visit our website, www.garethstevens.com. For a free color catalog of all our high-quality books, call toll free 1-800-542-2595 or fax 1-877-542-2596.

Library of Congress Cataloging-in-Publication Data

Names: Mikoley, Kate, author.
Title: Be a mentor! / Kate Mikoley.
Description: New York : Gareth Stevens Publishing, [2019] | Series: Be the change! shaping your community | Includes index.
Identifiers: LCCN 2017046109| ISBN 9781538220078 (library bound) | ISBN 9781538220092 (pbk.) | ISBN 9781538220108 (6 pack)
Subjects: LCSH: Mentoring–Juvenile literature.
Classification: LCC BF637.M45 M55 2018 | DDC 158.3–dc23 LC record available at https://lccn.loc.gov/2017046109

First Edition

Published in 2019 by
Gareth Stevens Publishing
111 East 14th Street, Suite 349
New York, NY 10003

Designer: Laura Bowen
Editor: Joan Stoltman

Photo credits: Cover, p. 1 (main) stockyimages/Shutterstock.com; cover, p. 1 (background) PAKULA PIOTR/Shutterstock.com; pp. 4–5 kali9/E+/Getty Images; p. 6 JStone/Shutterstock.com; p. 7 kupicoo/E+/Getty Images; pp. 8, 29 Iakov Filimonov/Shutterstock.com; p. 9 Dragon Images/Shutterstock.com; p. 10 Rawpixel.com/Shutterstock.com; p. 11 Chris Baldwin/Image Source/Getty Images; pp. 12–13, 25 (community) wavebreakmedia/Shutterstuck.com; p. 15 Sergey Novikov/Shutterstock.com; p. 16 Lisa F. Young/Shutterstock.com; pp. 17, 25 (family) Africa Studio/Shutterstock.com; p. 19 Marc Romanelli/Blend Images/Getty Images; p. 21 Image Source/DigitalVision/Getty Images; p. 23 Marc Dufresne/E+/Getty Images; p. 25 (team, class) Monkey Business Images/Shutterstock.com; p. 25 (friend) CREATISTA/Shutterstock.com; p. 27 Orlando Sentinel/Contributor/Tribune News Service/Getty Images.

Printed in the United States of America

CPSIA compliance information: Batch #CS18GS: For further information contact Gareth Stevens, New York, New York at 1-800-542-2595.

CONTENTS

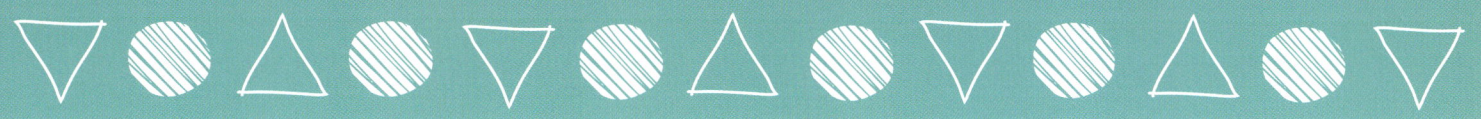

Words in the glossary appear in **bold** type the first time they are used in the text.

What's a Mentor?

Do you have someone you look to for help? Maybe your teacher is great at giving advice. Perhaps your brother helps you learn to play sports. Or maybe you have a friend in your class that helps you read. A mentor is a person who teaches things to another person or gives them help, support, and advice. These people are all mentors to you.

Find Your Fit

Mentors have more experience than the person they're helping. If there's something a person really enjoys or is especially good at, they can mentor others in that skill. But you don't have to have any special skills to be a mentor! Mentors also help people learn how to be good friends and help others.

You can be a mentor, too! Have you ever helped a friend learn something new? Maybe you're already a mentor and you don't even know it. Read on to discover how you can become a great mentor.

Mentors are often older than their mentee, or person being mentored, but not always. You can be a mentor to someone your own age—or even someone older than you!

Role Models

A mentor should be a positive role model. A positive role model is a person whose good behavior can be **imitated** by others. These are usually people who are **admired** by others for some reason. A role model can be someone you know, like your mentor, or they can be a public figure.

Mentors are usually role models, but role models don't have to be mentors. The main difference between the two is that a mentor is someone you communicate with. A role model can be a person you don't even know, such as a famous basketball player or a well-known scientist.

Malala Yousafzai

Malala Yousafzai, a young girl from Pakistan, is a positive role model to many people. In some parts of the world, girls still don't have all the same rights boys do. At a young age, Malala risked her life to fight for education for girls in her country and around the world.

Malala can't be a mentor to everyone who looks up to her. Mentors usually help people who live in their community or who they can regularly talk to over the phone or internet.

7

If you have a younger brother or sister, they probably look up to you. This means they admire you and pay close attention to the things you do. You're their role model! You can help them by setting a good example. You might already feel this is part of your responsibilities as an older **sibling.** Your parents might even have said they expect it of you. It's good practice for being a mentor.

Have you ever noticed your little brother or sister copying the things you do? That's because they want to be just like you! If you set a good example, they'll follow.

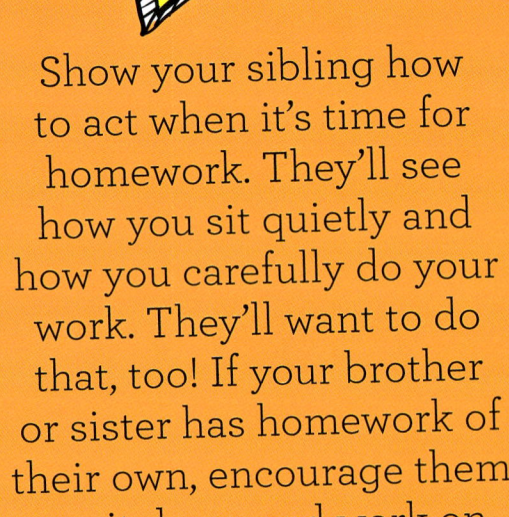

Your Turn!

Show your sibling how to act when it's time for homework. They'll see how you sit quietly and how you carefully do your work. They'll want to do that, too! If your brother or sister has homework of their own, encourage them to sit down and work on it while you do yours.

You can show your sibling how to play nicely, too!

Ask for Help

Mentors are leaders, but even leaders need help sometimes. Getting started as a mentor might seem hard, but with help, it doesn't have to be. An adult might be able to help you find mentoring opportunities. Ask a parent or teacher if they know of any places you could get started.

A volunteer is someone who chooses to do something without getting paid for their work. Most mentors are volunteers. An adult might know of programs in your community or school where you could volunteer to help people. They can help you get **involved** in these programs.

Your Turn!

Many places offer mentoring programs. For example, dance schools often have programs for older dancers to help newer dancers. Make a list of places in your community that might have these types of programs. Then look online to see if the places on your list have any mentoring opportunities.

Mentoring someone in something you already love is a great way to get started. You'll have fun while sharing your skill with others!

11

Be a Buddy at School!

There are probably many ways for you to get involved with mentoring in your community right now. Your school is a great place to start!

Do you like to read? You might be great at mentoring in your school's "reading buddies" program.

Your school might already have a reading buddies program. If so, ask a teacher how you can join. If your school doesn't have one, you can ask a teacher if they can help you start one. Some local libraries also have reading buddies programs in which you can volunteer!

These mentoring opportunities will pair you with a younger student. Then you'll help your reading buddy practice reading. You'll have lots of fun helping someone who is new to going to school, and you'll be helping them make a friend and learn how to get along with others. Many mentors consider their mentees to be close friends!

Some reading buddies meet in groups instead of pairs. A group could have many mentors and mentees all reading together.

Many mentors are older than their mentees, but that doesn't always have to be the case. Schools sometimes have different types of groups where students help other students. These can be called peer-mentoring programs. Many of these kinds of programs meet after school.

Sometimes people in peer-mentoring programs can help each other with homework. They might also help each other with personal or social problems. Some things can be easier to talk about with someone your own age, rather than with an adult. These programs can help you meet great people. You'll make friends with people you might otherwise never have met!

Cross-Age Peer Mentoring

Cross-age peer mentoring is the term used for programs where older students help younger students, such as reading buddies programs. Cross-age programs are considered peer mentoring because they still involve young people helping other young people, even if they aren't exactly the same age.

Some people prefer their mentors to be their peers because it can be more like just being with a friend. An older mentor might seem like an authority figure.

15

If you've ever had to **transfer** schools, you know how scary it can be. Even if you haven't, you can probably imagine how hard it might be.

In some schools, new students get paired up with a student who has gone there for a while. This helps the new student **adjust** to the changes they're facing. The student who's not new can be a mentor, but more importantly, they can be a friend to the new student and help them make more friends. They can also help the new student find their way around and get comfortable in the new setting.

Your Turn!

Your school might not have this kind of mentor program, but you can still help! If there's a new kid in your class, **introduce** them to your friends. Many schools are very different, so you can answer questions they have about your school and show them where everything is.

Your teacher might have different rules than your new friend had at their old school. They might do other things differently, too. You can help them learn!

In the Community

Many community programs need mentors. Your library or a community center might be a good place for you to start looking. These places may have programs you can join now, like a reading buddies program.

However, some of these kinds of programs have age **requirements**. A mentor may have to be an adult, or at least a high school student. If that's the case, don't worry about it. You can still ask questions and try to find out as much about the program as possible. It's never too early to start learning about becoming a mentor.

Tutors

A tutor is a person who teaches a student one-on-one. Mentors are different than tutors because they help with more than homework. At the Learning Buddies program in Seattle, Washington, mentors help their buddies learn math by playing games. Mentees learn important skills they need for school while having fun!

If your library has a mentoring program, the librarian might be able to help answer questions you have about it.

19

Some community mentoring programs pair children with an adult volunteer who can be their mentor. This adult acts as a role model to the child. They spend a **scheduled** amount of time together and often build **meaningful** friendships with each other that last beyond their years in the program. They may go on outings or just hang out. Groups such as the Boys & Girls Clubs of America and the YMCA often offer these types of programs.

Some of these programs bring a bunch of mentors and mentees together to do fun activities, such as bowling, ice skating, or to volunteer at places like soup kitchens. In addition to building a great mentor-mentee relationship, these programs allow people to make even more friends.

Big Brothers Big Sisters

Big Brothers Big Sisters is a well-known mentoring program across the country. Adult volunteers are called "bigs," while the kids they mentor are called "littles." Bigs and littles usually spend a few hours together every couple weeks. They can watch a baseball game, make art, eat a meal together, and more!

There are many other programs out there similar to Big Brothers Big Sisters. You can learn about them now so you're ready to volunteer when you're old enough.

21

Be a Mentee

One of the best ways to learn how to be a mentor is to have one of your own. Chances are good that you already have a mentor in your life! Maybe your soccer coach helps you learn new skills or your aunt has been teaching you how to cook. These people could be your mentor.

It's OK if you can't think of a person who's already your mentor. Ask a parent or teacher if they can help you get involved in a program like the ones talked about in this book. Once you have a mentor of your own to spend time with, you can learn what they do from your experiences with them.

Your Turn!

Pay attention to how your mentor helps you. Ask questions and let them tell you about the ways they try to be a good mentor. Watching and learning from someone who does what you want to do is a great way to add and grow skills. Sometimes this can be called apprenticing.

One way mentors sometimes teach their mentee new things is by playing a game. Games can be a fun way to learn!

23

Many Mentors and Mentees

There's no limit on how many mentors a person can have or on how many mentees one can have! If your mom is a manager at a bank, she might act as a mentor to some of the people who work there. She may also mentor people at your church.

Being a mentor is fun and rewarding, but it can also be hard. When a mentor first starts, it's a good idea for them to only mentor one person. Mentors need to remember to take time for themselves, too. Mentors won't be able to be very good helpers if what they're doing is making them tired or anxious.

Mentors in the Movies

Mentors and mentees are often shown in books and movies. In the Harry Potter stories, the main character, Harry, had several mentors, including Professor Dumbledore, Hagrid, some older classmates, and some of his teachers. Harry was also a mentor to some of his classmates.

WHO TO MENTOR

TEAMMATES

FAMILY MEMBERS

FRIENDS

PEOPLE-IN-THE COMMUNITY

CLASSMATES

Can you think of other people you could be a mentor for?

Be a Good Mentor

There are a few things you need to keep in mind when looking for a person to mentor. One of the most important things is to remember to make sure the person you'd like to mentor wants your help. Some people prefer learning on their own, and you don't want to push yourself into someone's life. Sometimes it's better to just be friends with someone instead of being their mentor.

Another thing to remember is that mentors should help build their mentee's **confidence**. A good mentor never makes their mentee feel bad for not knowing things that the mentor already knows.

The Astronaut's Mentor

Sally Ride was the first American woman in space. She was also a professor who helped many in science and math. Her mentor was one of her professors, Dr. Arthur Walker. Ride once said of Walker, "He **instilled** confidence, and made me believe that I could accomplish what I set out to accomplish."

Sally Ride inspired and helped many people. She came up with a NASA program that allows middle school students to take pictures of Earth using a camera in space!

Looking Forward

If you enjoy being a mentor, there are some careers you might be interested in when you're older. People with strong mentoring skills often become teachers or coaches. Perhaps one of these jobs is right for you. Maybe you prefer the idea of volunteering.

Whether you think you're ready to be a mentor right now or not, there's plenty you can do to get ready. Most importantly, try to set a good example and be helpful whenever possible. The best mentors always try to do what they think is right. Sometimes they're not even trying to be a mentor—it just happens!

Get the Grade

Good mentors are often good students. This doesn't necessarily mean you have perfect grades. It means you work hard, are nice to classmates, go to school regularly, and take part in activities. You don't have to be perfect to be a mentor. What matters is that you always try your best!

START NOW!

Set a good example for your friends and younger family members.

Ask an adult if they can help you find places and ways to be a mentor.

Introduce yourself to new people at school.

Be helpful and friendly.

Get your own mentor and learn from them.

Here's a list of things you can start doing now to get ready to be a mentor.

GLOSSARY

adjust: to make something fit

admire: to respect or think highly of someone

confidence: a feeling or belief that one can do something well or succeed

imitate: to copy

instill: to gradually cause someone to have a particular attitude or feeling

introduce: to make someone known to someone else by name

involve: to take part in something

meaningful: having real importance or value

requirement: something that is necessary for something else to happen or be done

schedule: to do the same things at the same time regularly

sibling: a brother or sister

transfer: to move from one place to another

FOR MORE INFORMATION

BOOKS

Antill, Sara. *10 Ways I Can Help My Community.* New York, NY: PowerKids Press, 2012.

Parker, Vic. *Inspiring Others.* Chicago, IL: Heinemann Library, 2013.

Raum, Elizabeth. *Helping Others.* Chicago, IL: Heinemann Library, 2013.

WEBSITES

Big Brothers Big Sisters of America
www.bbbs.org
Learn more about this mentoring program, and find out how you might be able volunteer for it when you're older.

Kids Are Heroes
www.kidsareheroes.org
Find out how kids just like you are making a difference in the world.

INDEX